CONTENTS

INTRODUCTION

You are clinging to a cliff high above the ground. Sweat is pouring down your face, even though the wind is bitterly cold. You look for your next move. Do you step up, to the right, or to the left? Your fingers ache as you make your choice. To some people, this situation is not a nightmare but the thrill that draws them to the extreme sport of climbing.

Rock climbing and ice climbing have a simple goal: to get from the bottom of a surface to the top. There are no other rules. However, no one would say that either sport is easy. In fact, both can be incredibly dangerous. In order to safely participate, climbers need skill, knowledge, and experience. Climbing equipment, though not always necessary, can be the difference between life and death.

Rock climbers and ice climbers do have opponents. One is nature itself—the surface they are climbing. They need to use it to make their way to the top, though it may seem as smooth as glass at times. Sometimes, climbers will have to battle harsh weather conditions, too. A climber has another opponent—himself or herself. Climbing challenges an individual's strength, courage, and problem-solving skills. Photographs of climbers seeming to hang by their fingertips

Every foot and hand placement is important in climbing. Each brings you one step closer to the ultimate goal: an extreme height or a beautiful view.

dazzle beginners and remind them of the sport's risky demands on the human body.

Climbing resembles other sports in that people often climb as teams. Each member relies on other team members, not just to get to their goal, but also to keep them safe from harm. Competitive climbing also requires great speed.

This book will introduce newcomers to the world of climbing. It is not a manual but a starting point. Those interested in these daring sports will learn what steps to take to get into climbing themselves. These activities may seem daunting at times, but it is important to remember that every climber had to begin somewhere.

CHAPTER ONE

UP FOR THE CHALLENGE

The inspiration for the sports of rock climbing and ice climbing may come from mountaineering, or mountain climbing, which people did not practice as a sport until modern times. Mountaineering means attempting to reach the highest point on a mountain.

Years ago, some people climbed mountains for religious reasons, believing the mountains were a spiritual place. Others climbed to reach a vantage point to observe surrounding lands and neighboring countries. And, of course, sometimes climbing mountains was the shortest route from one place to another—even if not the easiest.

Mountains were also a place of interest for scientists studying life at high altitudes, collecting rock and mineral samples, and gathering data about weather and climate. In fact, it was a scientist who probably set in motion the sport of mountaineering.

CONQUERING THE HEIGHTS

In 1760, Swiss scientist Horace Bénédict de Saussure offered a reward to anyone who could climb the tallest peak in Europe,

Mont Blanc in the Alps. Twenty-five years later, Dr. Michel-Gabriel Paccard and his porter, Jacques Balmat, finally succeeded. By the mid-1800s, other climbers were endeavoring to climb similar and taller peaks.

After the world's tallest mountains were conquered—including the highest of all, Mount Everest in the Himalayas in 1953 at 29,035 feet (8,850 meters)—mountaineers wanted greater challenges. So, they began trying more difficult routes. By the 1960s, this meant scaling sheer rock and ice surfaces with the aid of new tools and advanced climbing techniques. The sports of rock climbing and ice climbing were thus born.

A bronze statue of Michel-Gabriel Paccard stands in France, a lasting reminder of the great feat he accomplished with Jacques Balmat.

KINDS OF ROCK CLIMBING

Today's rock climbing is often divided into categories that require different skills and, sometimes, equipment. Traditional (or "trad") climbing is what most people think of when they picture rock climbing.

Also sometimes called technical climbing, teams of climbers are connected by rope as they scale surfaces. They place anchors, or pieces of protection, in the rock face through which rope is drawn to protect them in the event of a fall.

Sport climbing is similar to trad climbing except the anchors, also called "pro," are already placed in the rock. This allows climbers to make it up to the top faster and without having to buy or carry pro. Sport climbing is a bit safer, too, since the pieces of protection are anchored by professionals and meant to be used over a long period of time.

Bouldering is the sport of climbing large rocks called boulders. Since boulders are usually not too high, boulderers often do not use rope. They go only as high as they can jump down safely. However, they may place a "crash pad" below in case they fall. Far from being easy, bouldering is a great way to learn about the difficulties of moving on a rock surface without worrying about a lot of equipment.

A boulderer practices his moves on a rock by the ocean. If he cannot reach the top, he will jump safely back onto the sand.

Bouldering is a form of free climbing. Free climbing is the most dangerous rock climbing. Free climbers use no ropes or protective gear to help them climb or support their weight. They have only their skills and strength to get them up a rock surface. When high up on a rock face, any slip or fall can have terrible consequences for a free climber.

TIME TO CLIMB

Rock climbing and ice climbing expeditions are not always meant to take a few hours or even a single day. Some take several days, weeks, or months. Climbers may leave ropes and equipment in place and climb down each night to return in the morning. Or, they may spend days on the route until they can finish the climb. Sometimes storms and other weather conditions can make a journey take much, much longer.

In 1970, climbing partners Warren Harding and Dean Caldwell spent twenty-seven days trad climbing an unconquered face of the granite monolith El Capitan in the Sierra Nevada. The two men had planned to climb the 3,000-foot (914 m) surface, called the Dawn Wall, over twelve days. However, rain and freezing temperatures slowed them down. At one point, the National Park Service wanted to rescue the two hanging climbers, but they refused. They hauled up food and took nearly four weeks to complete the expedition, but they finally made it.

In early 2015, Tommy Caldwell and Kevin Jorgeson took nineteen days to complete the first free climb of the Dawn Wall.

ICE CLIMBING CONDITIONS

An ice climber in Alberta, Canada, is up to the challenge of scaling this frozen waterfall, an example of water ice.

Ice climbers may trad climb or free climb, but an added challenge in this sport is the different kinds of ice environments. Alpine ice starts as snow, usually on top of a mountain, and becomes hard-packed ice. It is sometimes called blue ice. Ice climbers may have to scale a mountain just to reach blue ice.

There is also water ice, which can form from frozen runoff or a water feature. For example, some ice climbers love scaling frozen waterfalls. The advantage of climbing water ice is that the surface may be easier to reach than alpine ice. However, these ice features are usually so vertical that the climb is exceptionally difficult. The quality of the ice also changes within a season or even a day.

Many routes in nature include both rock and ice. These are called mixed routes, and mixed climbers must be ready for the challenges of both surfaces. This calls for using both rock and ice climbing equipment and techniques, highlighted in the next chapters.

CHAPTER TWO

EQUIPPED AND READY

The body is the most important climbing tool. Hands are mostly used for balance. The feet support the body, and the legs are usually the source of strength. Climbers' eyes continuously scan the environment, looking for nooks, cracks, or ledges (called handholds and footholds) in which to put their hands and feet.

This climber tests his handhold with his weight before moving his feet up.

The general rule is to maintain three points of contact on the rock face at all times. This way, climbers can test the next hold while retaining a firm position. If the hold does not seem firm and steady, they can try another place without feeling desperate.

While bouldering and free climbing require less equipment than traditional rock climbing and ice climbing, all climbers need some gear to help them overcome their route. Most rock climbers and ice climbers depend on some essential tools to get them safely where they want to go.

THE ROPE

Rope is literally the climbers' lifeline. They cannot use just any rope, even if it is thick. Climbing rope is specially made for this sport. Dynamic rope has elasticity, or stretchiness. The elasticity can absorb the force of a great fall. However, a static rope is much stiffer. It is used in situations in which climbers do not want bounce, such as rescues and descents.

Climbers should make sure their rope has met the requirements of an official climbing organization. In order to meet these regulations, ropes must, among other things, be able to handle a certain number of falls and reach a certain length when stretched. Obviously, a climber wants a rope long enough to help him or her reach the top but not to hit the ground if falling.

A harness should fit snugly but not be too tight. This harness has extra loops to attach gear.

GETTING DRESSED

Usually, the rope ties into a nylon harness that fits tightly over a climber's hips. The harness often has leg loops that circle each leg as well. There is a place to tie the rope onto the front of the harness. The harness must be buckled or fastened correctly and securely or it may not hold during a fall. Gear can be clipped to the waist belt of the harness for easy access.

KNOTTY KNOWLEDGE

There are many kinds of knots used in climbing, and learning to tie them correctly is a key skill. The figure-eight follow-through knot (also called the Flemish bend and figure-eight trace knot) is one of the most common climbing knots and is used to tie the rope into a harness. Here is how to master this knot:

- **Start with rope about an arm's length long and make a loop at the top of the rope.**
- **Make a twist.**
- **Take the tail end of the rope around and go up through the loop to make a figure eight.**
- **Use the tail end of the rope to attach to the climbing harness (as directed in the harness handbook).**
- **Go back and follow the exact path of the first figure eight.**
- **Leave a tail about 3 to 6 inches (7.6 to 15 centimeters) long.**

Rock climbing shoes are also essential. These shoes have little padding but provide plenty of friction on the rock's surface so that climbers can use their feet in different ways to aid their climb. These ways include edging, or using the side of the shoe to stand on a foothold, and frictioning, which means putting the whole foot flat against the rock. Regular sneakers or shoes would be too slippery. Climbers keep their shoes in good condition by putting them on only at the site; they do not even walk from their cars in them.

Climbers also wear special helmets made from plastic or fiberglass. Not only are climbing helmets meant to cushion the head in case of a fall, but they also protect it from debris dropping from above. The helmet should be snug and fit just over the eyebrows. Helmets, too, are tested by professional climbing organizations to ensure quality.

All climbers, including free climbers, use chalk on their hands to get a better grip on the surface. A strenuous, sometimes nerve-wracking sport like climbing makes the body sweat—including the palms of the hands. Chalk can absorb perspiration. Chalk comes in different colors to match the color of the rock being climbed, leaving less of an impact on the environment. It can be carried as a loose powder in a bag hanging from a harness or as a chalk ball, often used for indoor walls.

HANG ON

Carabiners are metal rings with "gates" that open and shut. They can be a few shapes, including oval and D-shaped. Climbers use different types, depending on the situation. Some carabiners with locking gates are needed for times in which it would be deadly if the carabiner opened and released the climbing rope, for example. But some nonlocking carabiners are needed for ease of use, such as when only one hand is available to retrieve gear on the harness attached by the carabiner.

A carabiner that attaches to an anchor should be thick to support the body's weight, if needed.

A quick draw consists of a sewn nylon extension connecting two carabiners. Quick draws are vital for sport-climbing routes and useful for traditional climbing. They are designed to attach the rope to pieces of protection during a climb. The top carabiner can move freely on the anchor and act as a hinge. The bottom carabiner allows for easy rope attachment.

There are several names for the gear used in conjunction with rope and carabiners, including protection, pro, and anchors. The name "protection" is descriptive, though, as they hold the climber's body or his or her rope to the climbing surface. In sport climbing, these anchors are already fixed on the face, but in trad climbing, climbers must find the right spot and place them securely so that the downward force of a falling body would not dislodge it. These tools are placed in cracks or holes and—when used correctly—provide a stable place for a climber to attach the rope. There are two categories of protection: active and passive. Active pro have movable pieces, such as spring-loaded parts that can be made to fit in different sized cracks. Passive pro are pieces of metal with no movable parts. Pieces of pro include pitons, chocks, cams, wedges, stoppers, and hexes.

JUST ADD ICE

Ice climbers have a different set of challenges that call for specialized equipment. An ice tool, or ice axe, is one of their essential instruments. The ice tool has a head with two sides. One side is a sharp pick, which is swung into ice and snow and used as a hook. The other side, the adze, is more like a shovel. It is used to cut steps into ice. The ice tool may have a hole in its head so that it can remain attached to the climber using a leash. The metal shaft of the ice tool sometimes ends in a sharp spike so the tool can be used as a pole to stick into the ground surface when hiking.

On a sheer ice surface such as this, with few handholds and footholds, two shorter ice tools are needed for upward movement.

The size of the ice tool depends on the size of the climber. It can be as long as 2 feet (61 cm). However, the common rule is that climbers spending time on lower-angle terrain should use a longer ice tool. Steeper terrains require shorter axes, and the climber will need one for each arm.

Rock climbing shoes or winter boots will not work well on ice-climbing surfaces, so ice climbers wear leather or synthetic boots onto which they strap crampons. Crampons usually have ten to fourteen steel points, or spikes, for exceptional grip on slippery surfaces.

Ice climbers also need special pieces of protection. Ice screws are threaded tubes that can be twisted into an ice surface. As in rock climbing, the ice screw and an attached quick draw and rope keep an ice climber from falling too far. Interestingly, ice climbers can even carve their own anchors in ice, called bollards, though this takes time.

No matter what the surface of the climb or the gear they carry, all master climbers give it their all to make it to the top. Read on to learn their most common methods of conquering the climb.

CHAPTER THREE

TACKLING THE WALL

Some climbers do research before a climb. They get tips from others about how to tackle a wall and perhaps about a certain route to take. Others prefer to climb without any prior knowledge. It all depends on the level of difficulty the climber is looking for.

Techniques of climbing vary depending on the kind of climbing one does. Sport climbers do not need to worry about pieces of protection—they are already fixed to the wall, usually drilled in for maximum safety. Free climbers do not worry about protection either. They use only their hands and some chalk, after all. But sport climbers, trad climbers, and ice climbers in the outdoors may share some of the same methods to achieve their goals.

LEAD CLIMBING

In lead climbing, participants act as a team. One person takes the role of lead climber, and another is called the belayer. The

The belayer must be aware of the lead's movements at all times. A climb like this would be much more dangerous without a belayer.

leader is the more experienced climber. The lead climber has the rope attached to his or her harness, while the other end of the rope is run through a belay device on the harness of the belayer. Belay devices act like brakes on the rope. When climbers move in pairs, one climber uses this device to keep the rope attached to the other climber snug. As the lead climber ascends, the belayer allows rope out. The two climbers are connected in this way at all times.

As the lead climbs, he or she looks for edges and hollows in the rock surface that can act as handholds and footholds. Every few feet, he or she places a piece of protection in the rock and clips in with a quick draw. This protection now acts as an anchor. Should the lead climber fall, he or she will still be attached to the last anchor through which the climbing rope was threaded and can fall only a certain distance. The belayer is always watching from below to put the brake on the belaying device so more rope cannot escape if there is a fall. The belay device also helps absorb the falling force.

The lead climber climbs about as high as half the length of the team's rope, often about 75 to 90 feet (23 to 27 meters) and securely anchors in to a ledge or other safe place. Then, the belayer starts to climb, and the leader acts as the belayer, ready for any falls. When the belayer reaches a piece of pro the lead climber placed, he or she removes it. When the lead climber and the belayer reach each other on a climb, they are said to have completed one "pitch." It may take many pitches to get to the top.

KEY COMMUNICATION

Communication is key between leaders and belayers. When beginners take lessons, they are often instructed about certain short phrases to use so there are no misunderstandings between partners. Here are some:

"Take!" or "Take in!"	The belayer should make the rope to the leader tighter.
"Slack!"	The leader wants more rope.
"On belay!"	The leader is safe.
"Climb when ready!"	The belayer can start to climb.
"Watch me!"	The climber might be in trouble. Be ready to act.
"OK!"	The listener heard and understood.

TOP ROPING

Top roping is an ideal way to "try out" trad climbing maneuvers without worrying about placing pro. In top roping, a fixed anchor is at the top of the wall. The end of the climbing rope is threaded through the top anchor, through the climber's harness, and then ends with the belayer on the ground. The leader can climb safely, searching for handholds and footholds without considering further protection placement.

The belayer's job is still an important one. Some belayers even tie themselves to the ground, fearing the force of the leader's fall could drag them up the cliff. Once the pitch is over, the belayer may lower the lead climber to the ground.

In this situation, the security of the top anchor is imperative. In some places, it may be professionally anchored. Other people use trees as anchors or set their own. The anchor should always be inspected thoroughly. Even then, a backup anchor is a great way to ensure safety.

SPORT CLIMBING

Sport climbing can be top roped as well and is often indoors, but it allows the climber to learn what it is like to hook in to protection that has been preplaced on a route. Sport climbers tend to be speedy, and though they fall a lot, they often need to perform some amazing maneuvers just to hook into the next anchor. Sport climbing routes are often placed on surfaces that would be impossible to lead climb on.

Sport climbing is growing in popularity because it can be done indoors and outdoors. Climbers can practice leading without being an expert on placing pro. It is also a rapidly expanding competitive sport.

ICE AT AN ANGLE

Ice climbing techniques depend on the terrain. On low-angled slopes, many use flat footing, also called the French technique. In this method, the climber walks somewhat like a duck and places all crampon points flat on ice. On higher-angled slopes, the climber sidesteps. Ice climbers may still use handholds instead of their ice tools at these angles.

On steep or vertical surfaces, front pointing—or the German technique—is employed. This involves using the front points of the

ICE-COLD CLIMBING MOVES

Cane	Use ice tool like a cane when traveling on mostly flat terrain
Cross-body	Sidestep and turn body sideways to slope
Monkey Hang	While hanging on tools, transfer weight from arm muscles to bones to save strength
Fang	Ice climb with no hand tools, only gloves and handholds
Piolet Traction	Place an ice tool above the head and pull down on the shaft to provide a handhold
Traverse	Move sideways on the ice face

crampons to step up. It is also necessary to use ice tools, however. Swinging an ice tool to achieve a secure "stick" can be difficult. Bad swings cause ice to break, and multiple swings can tire the arm. But with practice, beginning ice climbers get a feel for it.

On steep surfaces, instructors suggest ice climbers keep their bodies in a triangular shape, with their legs wider than their shoulders. As they move up, they should establish secure footing, sometimes kicking several times into the ice with their crampons. Next, they swing their ice tool with their arm fully extended. When they get a good stick, they swing and stick the other ice tool. Then, climbers lift themselves to about eye height on the tool head, find good footing, and start again. If they are lead climbing, they may place an ice screw as protection at points along the way.

DESCENT

No matter how climbers get there, it is impressive to enjoy the view from the top and the feeling of accomplishment that accompanies such an athletic feat. However, no climbing expedition is done until everyone reaches the bottom safely. It is sometimes possible to hike down. However, some climbers may not have a choice: They have to descend the same way they came up.

There are a few ways climbers descend, and they may need to use more than one to get down. One method of descent is called down climbing. Down climbing is simply using one's hands and feet to descend. Some do not use a rope, which is very dangerous. On sport climbing surfaces, partners might lower each other down. The belayer uses the belaying device to lower the leader. On steep surfaces, however, it is often safer to rappel.

Rappelling (called abseiling outside the United States) is a controlled slide down a rope that has been anchored at the top of the climb. Climbers use a rappel device to help control the speed

A climber rappels down a steep rock face in South Africa. The safest rappelling requires a slow descent with as much contact with the wall as possible.

of descent. It is extremely important to keep one or both hands on the brake of the rappel device. Letting go can cause accidents. On the descent, the climber leans back in the harness, facing the wall, and uses his or her feet to "walk down" the surface. Descent should be steady and not too bouncy, which puts unwanted strain on the top anchor.

Rappelling is only for the most experienced climbers. Many accidents have occurred in rappelling situations because climbers are tired from the climb up and have not taken proper safety precautions.

CHAPTER FOUR

GETTING STARTED

If you are interested in rock or ice climbing, there are easy ways to gather knowledge about it before getting in a harness. First, read all about it. Public libraries have many books available for climbers of all levels. The Internet is another valuable source of both written information as well as instructive videos. However, there are many websites created by amateurs, so always be sure the advice offered is from a reputable source or organization. After the research, it is time to build muscles and skills.

GETTING FIT

Much of climbing is about developing strength and stamina. Climbers use every part of their bodies and sometimes find themselves in dangerous situations, holding on for their lives. So, it is important to get fit from head to toe.

The most basic skill of climbing is hiking, which is an activity anyone can do at a local park. Try choosing hiking trails that have hills. Most parks with

Some hiking trails offer challenging routes and amazing views. Hiking requires little gear, too.

trails have information about how challenging the trails are. State and national parks recommend hiking with a group or partner and, just like in climbing, it is always better to go with at least one experienced older person.

Advanced climbers may perform more exercises to develop their strength. They lift weights, run, and do pull-ups, push-ups, and sit-ups. They do these workouts often, as climbers have to use their muscles many times on their journey. Endurance is essential to experienced climbers.

A climbing gym is a great place to learn the tips and tricks of the pros. Beginners can receive instruction on the wall, too.

HIT THE INDOOR WALL

After starting an overall fitness routine, and before investing in expensive climbing gear, beginners should get a feel for the sport at an indoor climbing gym. Many of these places offer walls of varying difficulties, classes, and one-on-one training for climbers of all ages. Indoor climbing gyms provide a safer, more controlled environment to get accustomed to equipment, such as harnesses and ropes, and procedures, such as selecting handholds and footholds, belaying, and even knot tying. Protection is usually already on the wall and a top knot is often the anchor of choice.

Future ice climbers do not have to have their first experience outdoors, either. There are indoor ice walls, too. Scotland is home to the biggest indoor ice climbing arena in the world. Called the Ice Factor Kinlochleven, the center offers both ice climbing and rock climbing instruction to more than thirteen thousand visitors a year.

GETTING OUTSIDE

Gyms are a great place to start, but most outdoor climbers say there is no substitute for the real thing—the outdoor rock face. In addition to all the special climbing equipment, climbers need warm and windproof clothing that is easy to move in. If getting to the climb involves hiking, they will need GPS or a compass and map to find their way. A backpack may be needed to store gear such as a flashlight, sunglasses, sunscreen, and a first-aid kit. Long climbs may mean camp equipment such as tents and sleeping bags.

Unsurprisingly, ice climbers have to be prepared with even more gear. They must be very warmly dressed with gloves on their hands. They may need skis to get to their route and perhaps even bottled oxygen, depending on the altitude of their climb.

Ice climbers worry disturbed snow and loose ice on mountaintops can turn into avalanches, threatening to bury or knock them down. Deep crevasses may be hidden by snow layers. Even trickier, snow and ice conditions can change throughout the day, freezing and thawing, meaning pieces of protection may not remain fixed over a long period of time. Ice climbers must be sure of weather conditions during the duration of their climb and descent. First-aid kits, avalanche beacons, and GPS devices should all be a part of an ice climber's pack.

Those who have never climbed outside before should only do so with a reputable instructor. How do you know if he or she is reputable? Many instructors belong to respected organizations

RATING ROUTES

There is a way for climbers to make sure they do not get in over their heads and choose a climb that is too difficult. Different countries use different rating systems to rate the difficulty of a route. Here is one often used in the United States:

U.S. Yosemite Decimal Rating System

Class 1	Walking an established flat, easy trail.
Class 2	Hiking a steep incline, maybe using hands.
Class 3	Climbing a steep incline, rope may or may not be used, and hands used in climbing. A short fall is possible.
Class 4	Climbing steeper. Most people use rope due to potential long fall.
Class 5	Belayed roping with protection is required. A fall could be fatal.

Class 5 sub-categories

5.1–5.4	Easy	Climbing a steep section that has large handholds and footholds.
5.5–5.8	Intermediate	Small handholds and footholds. Strength and rock climbing skills required.
5.9–5.10*	Hard	Very few handholds and footholds.
5.11–5.12	Hard to difficult	No obvious hand holds or footholds. Vertical, has overhangs.
5.13–5.15	Very difficult	Surface smooth, vertical, has overhangs.

*To further define a route's difficulty, a subclassification system of letters (a, b, c, or d) is used for climbs 5.9 and higher.

Ice Climb Ratings*

Water ice (WI)	Water ice disappears during the warmer months of the year. The scale ranges from WI1 (not very steep) to WI7 (vertical or overhanging, and very dangerous).
Alpine ice (AI)	Alpine ice is permanent, like the ice found in high altitudes or in glaciers. The scale is similar to the scale for water ice, ranging from AI1 to AI7.
Mixed ice (M)	Mixed ice routes may contain ice, but are partly rock. The mixed climbing scale ranges from M1 to M13, and each grade is described compared to a Yosemite Decimal System rating (M1 is similar to a Yosemite rating of 5.5).

*See http://www.alpinist.com/p/climbing_notes/grades for more detailed ice climb ratings.

such as the American Mountain Guides Association. They are insured and have medical qualifications and permits to climb. They have proof of training and experience, records of any accidents on their expeditions, and lastly, referrals from clients and professionals.

Climbers should not make the mistake of thinking climbing at the gym is similar to climbing outside. And they should not rely on friends who say they know what they are doing. Instructors have hours and hours of teaching experience. Just having experience climbing is not the same as knowing how to teach.

Instructors can help every step of the way, from putting on safety equipment to choosing the best holds. But safety is always their main concern.

The best instructors show climbers how to practice extreme safety in their extreme sport. They recommend triple-checking knots, anchors, and other gear. That final check may confirm that an anchor is too loose or a knot has been made in fraying rope. These could have disastrous results.

Instructors may start out teaching beginners on a sport climbing surface, then have them graduate to a top-roping cliff, and finally let them get a taste of leading and belaying on a trad climb. There is no need to hurry from one level to the next, though. There is a lot to learn in every climbing situation. The fun is in the journey and the natural surroundings, not necessarily in finding the hardest way to get to the top.

CHAPTER FIVE

COMPETITION CLIMBING

Because rock climbing and ice climbing are skilled sports, it is not surprising that these activities are now the focus of many competitions. And because both are thrilling—sometimes breathtaking—to watch, the sports' fans are quickly multiplying.

According to the International Council for Competition Climbing (IFSC), the first climbing competitions took place in the 1940s in the former Soviet Union. They were based on speed, rather than route difficulty. But it was not until decades later when the sports began to take hold in other countries.

A FAST-GROWING INTERNATIONAL SPORT

In 1985, many of the world's best climbers were invited to the first SportRoccia lead climbing competition in Italy, in which competitors had to conquer a rock face within a set amount of time. It proved to be so popular that the next year ten thousand fans attended and numerous television stations broadcast the event. By the late 1980s, French indoor competitions had begun, as well as the World Cup of Lead and Speed climbing. In 1998, bouldering became its own discipline in the World Cup.

The Union Internationale des Associations d'Alpinisme (UIAA), or International Climbing and Mountaineering Federation, established an organization to train climbing officials and decide competition rules. In the 1990s, under the UIAA, the world championship began, occurring every two years. Today, up to sixty countries send participants. The annual world youth championship includes competitors from as many as fifty nations. These two competitions continue to be the most popular. Each continent takes a turn hosting. (The competitions take place indoors or on artificial structures to address concerns about the environmental impact of such major events.) The UIAA decided to hand off governing these championships to the International Federation of Sport Climbing (IFSC) in 2007. However, the UIAA still oversees the Ice Climbing World Cup, which is held every two years, as well as the Ice Climbing World Championships, both youth and adult.

Today's IFSC rock climbing competitions are generally divided into three disciplines: speed, lead, and bouldering. In speed, competitors climb parallel walls, usually 49 feet (15 meters), while top roped. The fastest climber wins, often in a matter of several seconds. In lead competitions, athletes trad climb and are allowed eight minutes to

During the IFSC Boulder World Championships of 2014, more than two hundred athletes from forty-four countries participated in the men's and women's events.

climb as high as they can. In bouldering competitions, competitors get just ten movements to conquer their route.

The IFSC also oversees the Continental Championships and the annual World Cup circuit, which includes twenty-four events in lead, speed, and bouldering. In 2011, the Olympic Committee added sport climbing to a list of sports that may be added to the 2020 Olympic Games. Ice climbing, too, is in talks to become an Olympic sport in 2022.

ROCK STAR

Chris Sharma is often described as the world's best rock climber. He began rock climbing in his home state of California when he was twelve years old. He won a bouldering national championship at age fourteen. When he was fifteen, Sharma successfully tackled the hardest-ranked climb in North America, a 5.14c (the so-called Necessary Evil in the Virgin River Gorge between Utah and Arizona).

Since then, Sharma has conquered many other incredibly difficult routes around the world and won many competitions. He has been mentioned in several rock climbing documentaries. The 2007 movie *King Lines* focuses on Chris Sharma and his attempt to ascend Es Pontás, a natural arch off the island of Mallorca, Spain. He is the first and only person to do this.

USA CLIMBING

In the United States, the national governing body of competition climbing is USA Climbing. It promotes three kinds of climbing: bouldering, speed, and sport climbing. USA Climbing was originally a part of the American Sport Climbers Federation (ASCF). In 1998, it became an independent organization called the Junior Competition Climbing Association but expanded to include adult competitors in 2002 and adopted the name USA Climbing in 2003.

Today, USA Climbing oversees the American Bouldering Series, the Sport Climbing Series, and the Collegiate Climbing Series. Regional events for youth and adults lead to regional and national competitions and eventually world championships. Check out the organization's website at usaclimbing.net to find affiliated gyms and certified coaches.

JOIN THE CLIMBING CLUB

Those who are interested in rock climbing and ice climbing but are not quite ready to join a competitive league should consider joining a local club. Clubs can be great places for enthusiasts to socialize, share contacts, practice maneuvers both on and off the wall, and possibly organize expeditions outside together (with the help of a certified guide or instructor). Some high schools, colleges, and universities host clubs, as do many towns and cities. Doing an Internet search or looking for notices hung up around a local climbing gym are two ways of finding a club for both recreational and competitive climbing.

The number of climbing clubs is increasing, as is the number of climbers each year. According to the IFSC, three thousand people climb for the first time every day, and about twenty-five million

Climbing club members can share their experiences, ask questions, and discover valuable resources in their meetings. This club meets at an indoor gym where members will get hands-on instruction.

climb regularly. Climbers are not necessarily in mountain communities with outdoor climbing opportunities. London, England, has more than three hundred indoor walls. The United States has around six hundred climbing gyms today. Many climbers are young—about 39 percent are under the age of eighteen—and as many as 38 percent are female. Climbing is an activity for everyone.

Climbing is a complete sport. It takes muscle strength and endurance. It requires flexibility to get hands and feet into awkward holds. It challenges one's problem-solving skills, too. The way to the top is rarely straight up. Rock climbing and ice climbing, like all exercise, can even reduce stress. Few sports are as enjoyable or rewarding. Get to a gym and try it yourself!

GLOSSARY

avalanche A large amount of snow and ice or of dirt and rocks that slides suddenly down the side of a mountain.

beacon A device that transmits a radio signal so that someone can be found.

certified Proven that someone has met the requirements for or achieved a certain standard.

crampons A set of metal spikes fastened to the soles of boots or shoes to provide better traction.

crevasse A deep, narrow opening or crack in an area of thick ice or rock.

documentary A movie or television program presenting facts and information.

endurance The ability to sustain a prolonged stressful effort or activity.

GPS Global Positioning System; a navigational system using satellite signals to fix the location of a radio receiver on or above Earth's surface.

granite A very hard natural igneous rock formation of visibly crystalline texture.

incline A slanting surface.

maneuver A procedure or method of working, usually involving expert physical movement.

monolith A very large stone that is usually tall and narrow.

nylon A strong material that is made from a chemical process and that is used for making clothes, ropes, and other products.

porter A person employed to carry baggage.

reputable Respected and trusted by most people.

stamina Great physical strength that allows one to continue doing something for a long time.

synthetic Made by combining different substances. Not natural.

technique A way of doing something by using special knowledge or skill.

FOR MORE INFORMATION

Alpine Club of Canada (ACC)
201 Indian Flats Road
P.O. Box 8040 Stn Main
Canmore, AB T1W 2T8
Canada
(403) 678 3200 ext. 0
Website: http://www.alpineclubofcanada.ca

The ACC, the national mountaineering organization of Canada, is dedicated to preserving mountain environments as well as promoting mountain sports and other pursuits.

International Climbing and Mountaineering Federation (UIAA)
Monbijoustrasse 61 Postfach CH-3000
Bern 23
Switzerland
Website: http://www.theuiaa.org

The UIAA encourages the growth and protection of mountaineering and climbing worldwide. Founded in 1932, it has a presence on five continents with eighty member associations in fifty countries.

International Federation of Sport Climbing (IFSC)
Centro Arrampicata Torino
Via Paolo Braccini 18 10141
Torino, Italy
Website: http://www.ifsc-climbing.org

The IFSC is responsible for the direction, regulation, promotion, and development of climbing competitions worldwide.

Mountaineering Club of Alaska (MCA)
Box 243561
Anchorage, AK 99524-3561
Website: http://www.mtnclubak.org/index.cfm

The Mountaineering Club of Alaska supports mountaineering, hiking, climbing, and skiing and the preservation of the wilderness. The MCA also offers training events.

Ontario Climbing Federation
c/o True North Climbing Inc.
75 Carl Hall Road, Unit 14
Toronto, ON M3K 2B9
Canada
Website: http://www1.climbontario.ca
The Ontario Climbing Federation was established in 2011 and has youth membership opportunities as well as competitions.

USA Climbing
4909 Pearl East Circle, Suite 102
Boulder, CO 80301
(303) 499 0715
Website: http://usaclimbing.net/home.cfm
USA Climbing is the national governing body of competition climbing in the United States.It promotes competitions in bouldering, sport, and speed climbing.

WEBSITES

Because of the changing nature of Internet links, Rosen Publishing has developed an online list of websites related to the subject of this book. This site is updated regularly. Please use this link to access this list:

http://www.rosenlinks.com/STTE/Rock

FOR FURTHER READING

Benjamin, Daniel. *Extreme Rock Climbing*. New York, NY: Cavendish Square Publishing, 2014.

Cohn, Jessica. *Mountain Climbing*. New York, NY: Gareth Stevens Publishing, 2013.

Eng, Ronald C., and Julie van Pelt. *Mountaineering: The Freedom of the Hills*. Seattle, WA: Mountaineers Books, 2010.

Hill, Pete. *Indoor Climbing: Technical Skills for Climbing Walls for Novices, Experts, and Instructors*. Milnthorpe, England: Cicerone, 2009.

Rajczak, Kristen. *Climbing Mount Everest*. New York, NY: Gareth Stevens Publishing, 2014.

Shone, Rob, and Nik Spender. *Defying Death in the Mountains*. New York, NY: Rosen Central, 2010.

Takeda, Pete. *Climb: Your Guide to Bouldering, Sport Climbing, Trad Climbing, Ice Climbing, Alpinism, and More*. Clermont, FL: Paw Prints, 2008.

Young, Jeff C. *Belaying the Line: Mountain, Rock, and Ice Climbing*. Edina, MN: ABDO Publishing, 2011.

BIBLIOGRAPHY

Bouchard, Nancy Prichard. "Getting Started Rock Climbing." REI, February 18, 2014. Retrieved September 20, 2014 (http://www.rei.com/learn/expert-advice/getting-started-rock-climbing.html).

Brain, Marshall. "How Rock Climbing Works." HowStuffWorks.com. Retrieved September 2, 2014 (http://adventure.howstuffworks.com/outdoor-activities/climbing/rock-climbing1.htm).

Cinnamon, Jerry. *The Complete Climber's Handbook*. Camden, ME: Ragged Mountain Press, 2000.

Creasey, Malcolm. *Rock Climbing in a Weekend.* London, England: Anness Publishing, 2004.

Eiselt, Julie. "Belay Devices: How to Choose." REI, September 11, 2014. Retrieved September 19, 2014 (http://www.rei.com/learn/expert-advice/belay-device.html).

Green, Stewart. "4 Ways to Descend Cliffs and Mountains." AboutSports.com. Retrieved September 5, 2014 (http://climbing.about.com/od/cliimbingtechniques/a/4-Ways-To-Descend-Cliffs-And-Mountains.htm).

Green, Stewart. "How to Tie a Figure-8 Follow-Through Knot." AboutSports.com. Retrieved September 20, 2014 (http://climbing.about.com/od/climbingknots/ss/Figure8FollowTh.htm).

Gupta, Sameer. "10 Best Climbers That Shook the World." Camp Roxx, August 20, 2012. Retrieved September 13, 2014 (http://www.camproxx.com/10-best-rock-climbers-that-shook-the-world).

Kidd, Timothy, and Jennifer Hazelrigs, eds. *Rock Climbing.* Champaign, IL: Human Kinetics, 2009.

International Federation of Sport Climbing. "Climbing Competitions' History." IFSC-Climbing.org. Retrieved September 5, 2014 (https://www.ifsc-climbing.org/index.php/about-ifsc/what-is-the-ifsc/history).

Long, John. *How to Rock Climb!* Guilford, CT: The Globe Pequot Press, 2004.

McLellan, Dennis. "Warren J. Harding, 77; First Man to Scale Yosemite's El Capitan." *Los Angeles Times*, March 8, 2002. Retrieved September 10, 2014 (http://articles.latimes.com/2002/mar/08/local/me-harding8).

Mellor, Don. *Rock Climbing: A Trailside Guide*. New York, NY: W. W. Norton, 1997.

Ronca, Debra. "Can You Ice Climb a Waterfall?" HowStuffWorks.com. Retrieved September 5, 2014 (http://adventure.howstuffworks.com/outdoor-activities/climbing/waterfall-climbing1.htm).

Ronca, Debra. "How Ice Climbing Works." HowStuffWorks.com. Retrieved September 16, 2014 (http://adventure.howstuffworks.com/outdoor-activities/climbing/ice-climbing.htm).

Takeda, Peter. *Climb!* Washington, DC: National Geographic Society, 2002.

USA Climbing. "About USA Climbing." USAClimbing.net. Retrieved September 10, 2014 (http://usaclimbing.net/about_main.cfm).

Wise, Abigail. "How Rock Climbing Does Your Mind—and Body—Good." Huffington Post, August 30, 2014. Retrieved September 19, 2014 (http://www.huffingtonpost.com/2014/08/30/health-benefits-rock-climbing_n_5708847.html).

INDEX

ABOUT THE AUTHOR

Therese Shea, an author and former educator, has written over one hundred books for children and young adults on a variety of topics, including rock climbing, hiking, and camping, as well as written and edited several volumes on climbing Mount Everest. She holds English and education degrees from Providence College and the State University of New York at Buffalo. The author currently resides in Rochester, New York, with her husband, Mark.

PHOTO CREDITS

Cover, p. 4 My Good Images/Shutterstock.com; pp. 1, 3, 7, 12, 19, 27, 34 Vitalii Nesterchuk/Shutterstock.com; p. 5 Forest Woodward/Vetta/Getty Images; p. 8 Nando Machado/Shutterstock.com; p. 9 Jordan Siemens/The Image Bank/Getty Images; p. 11 Cory Richards/National Geographic Image Collection/Getty Images; p. 12 (inset) DreamPictures/Jensen Walker/Blend Images/Getty Images; p. 13 Cultura RM/Tim Hall/Getty Images; p. 15 Glowimages/Getty Images; p. 17 AlexSava/Vetta/Getty Images; p. 20 Jupiterimages/Stockbyte/Thinkstock; p. 25 Jack Ambrose/Stone/Getty Images; p. 27 (inset) Ascent Xmedia/The Image Bank/Getty Images; p. 28 Shane Hansen/E+/Getty Images; pp. 32–33 Daniel Milchev/Stone/Getty Images; p. 35 © AP Images; pp. 38–39 Hero Images/Getty Images; cover and interior pages graphics SkillUp/Shutterstock.com, Sfio Cracho/Shutterstock.com, saicle/Shutterstock.com, Frank Rohde/Shutterstock.com, Thomas Bethge/Shutterstock.com, nortivision/Shutterstock.com, PinkPueblo/Shutterstock.com.

Designer: Michael Moy; Editor: Shalini Saxena